THE CHRONICLES OF NOW

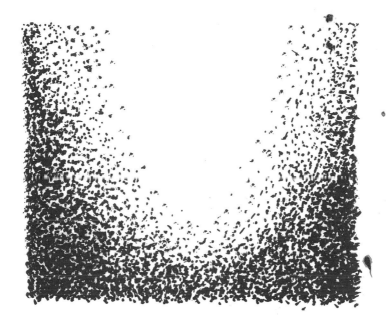

ANTHONY HADEN-GUEST

ALLWORTH
PRESS

School of
VISUAL ARTS

06   05   04   03   02   5   4   3   2   1

Published by Allworth Press
An imprint of Allworth Communications
10 East 23rd Street, New York, NY 10010

Copublished with The School of Visual Arts

Book design by James Victore, Inc.
Interior design and layout by Jennifer Moore and Matthew McGuiness,
James Victore, Inc.

Library of Congress Cataloging-in-Publication Data

Haden-Guest, Antony.
   The chronicles of now / Antony Haden-Guest.
      p. cm.
   ISBN 1-58115-220-5
   1. English wit and humor, Pictorial. I. Title.

NC1479.H25 A4 2002
741.5'942--dc21   2002022865

Printed in Canada

TABLE OF CONTENTS

CHAPTER

1

FEELINGS *1*

Affairs of the Heart, etc. *2*

What They Say & What They Mean: Advice to Lovers *18*

Postmodernist Excuses *20*

Not the 1000 Yards Stare: But Some Other Great Stares *24*

The Philosophy of Now:
Brand-New Proverbs for the 3rd Millennium *27*

CHAPTER

2

THE MIND AND ITS QUOTE UNQUOTE LIFE *45*

I loved Your Book:
And Other Good Stuff to Say to a Writer at His Party *56*

I Found It at the Movies: Some Helpful Hints *59*

Why & How I Make My Art *62* ◆ The Rhythm Section *66*

Evolution v. Creation *72*

CHAPTER

3

THE GOLDEN SECTION *75*

Celebrity is Revenge *76* ◆ Dangerous Minds *83*

What Were They Saying?:
The Good, the Bad and the Unbelievable *91*

Inside the Media Conspiracy *104*

What They Say & What They Mean: In the Tabloids *109*

Performer Anxieties *110*

CHAPTER

4

THE WAY WE LIVE NOW *113*

The Letter *114* ◆ Business Brains *115*

For Some Reason Simon's Normal Superb Communications Skills

Betrayed Him that Whole Long Frustrating Day *123*

Family Fun *126* ◆ His 'N' Hers Doormats *135*

What She Says & What She Means *136*

Modern Manners: Up the Down Staircase *138*

What They Say & What They Mean: At a Cocktail Party *162*

e-Answered Prayers *164* ◆ Notes Toward a New Etiquette *167*

The Class-War of Words *175*

Normal People! Journeys Into (Other People's) Space *178*

Some Highly Endangered Human Species *190* ◆ Closer to the Edge *195*

Happy Endings: Blueprint for an

End-of-the-World-as-We-Know-It Game *208*

INTRODUCTION

"The man who laughs has simply not yet heard the terrible news," wrote Bertolt Brecht. An odd observation, perhaps, from the man who wrote the book to the ferociously funny musical, *The Threepenny Opera*. One of the main functions of humor, after all, is to help us deal with the stuff we all go through, whether it be bruising, banal, embarrassing, peculiar, or, yes, terrible. You will find specimens of all categories within.

I owe a debt to Bill Beckley, who made the project possible, and to Tad Crawford, Jamie Kijowski, Michael Madole, Kate Lothman, James Victore and the others at Allworth Press, who made it actual. I am also grateful to those who have published the cartoons in the past from Tom Wolsey, who used them in *Town* magazine, to the late Bobby Birch of Britain's *Sunday Telegraph*, to Ed Kosner at *New York* magazine, to Arthur Carter and Peter Kaplan of the *New York Observer*, to Bruce Wolmer of *Art & Auction*, to Tina Brown and Maer Roshan for publishing "Dangerous Minds" in the ultimate issue of *Talk*,
and to Christopher Tennant for his labors on the project. I also want to thank those who have exhibited them, including the defunct nightclubs Kamikaze and Palladium, the vanished curator Christian Leigh (who put one—admittedly *hors de concours* into the 1993 Venice Biennale, of all places), Walter Robinson of ArtNet, the gallerists Charlie Finch, Melinda Hackett, Barbara Braathen, Amanda Obering, and Gottfried Tollman of Los Angeles, and—as I write—to Serge Sorokko in San Francisco and Jeffrey Deitch in New York.

A final point. Jacqueline Kennedy apparently once asked General de Gaulle which of the statesmen he had encountered had the greatest sense of humor. "Stalin, madame," de Gaulle answered. I later learned that Stalin would amuse himself during Politburo meetings by sketching cartoons of his soon-to-be victims. But he, of course, was making news, not hearing it.

—Anthony Haden-Guest

1

FEELINGS

I said feelings were important.
I didn't say *your* feelings were important.

AFFAIRS
OF THE HEART, ETC.

Joey doesn't kiss and tell. He kisses TO tell.

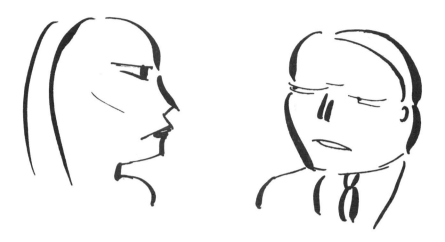

You mean you expect me to remember every teeny little promise?

But, Eddie, it never occurred to me you thought a date meant
a commitment for the *whole evening.*

You have a very old soul, Bunty.

Let's have lunch doesn't mean let's have lunch,
Bob. It means don't let's have dinner.

I know your time is precious, so I shall be succint. Fuck off!

They were married by the time Chloe found he'd lied about his age. He's only *seventy*.

I don't smoke. I'm a veggie. I've stopped using cellular phones.
Why in the world would I go to bed with you, Alex?

You can rely on Gwen.
She'll let you down every time.

Sorry. Herb. True, I am a slut.
But I have to draw the line somewhere.

Of course it was important for me, Alex.
For one thing, it really showed Fred!

I said I was worth millions. I didn't say I *had* millions.

I always think it's fate. And it's always a set-up.

No, I'm not your angel. I'm your angel's roommate.
Your angel is off on a toot with a boy angel.

It turned out it actually was a gun in his pocket.

So you're Cynthia. I hear you're a must.

Sure, it was with a perfect stranger.
But strangers are the only perfect people I know.

You see! Breaking up isn't so hard to do.

No, I'm just a sissy, I'm afraid.
That's like gay, but without the fun stuff.

We're all creatures of habit, Edwin. Mine is changing my mind.

I like you because you remind me of my mother.

If love is the answer, believe me, you're asking the wrong question.

I'm warm. You're fuzzy.
The whole thing was a hideous mistake.

Some things are too precious for money to buy.
I am not one of them.

I thought he was nice. But it turned out he was just lazy.

And if you aren't confused, Henry,
you simply haven't been paying attention.

Actually my memory is excellent. I forget you perfectly.

WHAT THEY SAY
& WHAT THEY MEAN

Advice to Lovers

The idea for What They Say & What They Mean came from the inimitable caricaturist, the late Mark Boxer.

She's a baby. I don't want you to be hurt.
*(I hope she ruptures your back, robs
you blind, gives you warts & runs off
with a ski instructor)*

You two are made for each other.
(You two deserve each other.)

She was always a free spirit.
(The slut!)

I knew the right person would come along.
(I give it a few months, tops)

I don't believe in being judgmental.
(Bleccthhh!)

Trust me.
*(Helllooo! National Enquirer?
Do I have a story for you?)*

POSTMODERNIST
EXCUSES

I'm terribly sorry...

… but I have to work on a fragrance.

… but my Fax was out of paper.

… but my mobile needs charging.

… but I have to rewind my videos.

… but you were deleted by a virus.

… but my Feng-Shui master said I should stay home.

NOT THE 1000 YARDS STARE

But Some Other Great Stares

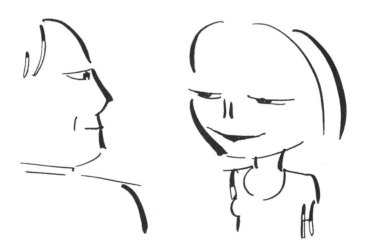

The Have-I-ever-got-the-goods-on-YOU, pal? stare.

The I-fear-I-may-be-going-mad stare.

The Do-you-realize-just-who-you-are-staring-at? stare.

The I-bet-you-wonder-why-I-always-give-you-this-thin-smile stare.

The I-know-you're-still-talking-because-I-can-see-your-lips-moving stare.

THE
PHILOSOPHY OF NOW

Brand-New Proverbs for the 3rd Millennium

There's no such thing as only a joke.

Don't throw the bathwater out with the baby.

Sometimes hell is *the same* people.

If at first you don't succeed – lower your standards.

What's the point of having a dream if it's not somebody else's nightmare?

The truth is a lie that hasn't been found out.

Beware! There's a fat man trying to get inside every thin woman!

Tattoos are *not* muscles.

Avoid pedophilia – the love that cannot spell its name.

At least tunnel vision is vision.

Rehab is for quitters!

We must tread the narrow line between right and wrong.

Why not eat the poor? There's more of them.

You *can* run and you *can* hide *and they may never catch you!*

Neon never lies!

Poison never dries!

Most rumors are true.

Whoever has nobody conspiring against them is failing in life.

Art isn't dead. It just smells funny.

Whatever does not kill you was probably just a preliminary bout

Never say never!

Oh, well! Being dysfunctional is better than not being functional at all.

You *can* judge a book by its cover.

The unlived life is not worth examining.

Tomorrow is another day. But so was yesterday.

Experience is what you get when you don't get what you want.

Nature may abhor a vacuum
but society adores one if she or he is cute enough.

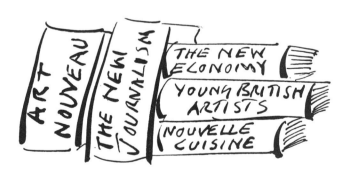

Embrace the New, wake up in bed with the Old.

Do not rely on Alternative Medicine unless you have an alternative body.

I forget where I got this. Apologies!

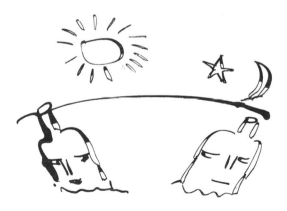

You have a Date with Destiny! You won't score.

There's something *really funny* about people who are always
smiling in their publicity photographs.

Even nice people usually have secret plans.

2

THE MIND AND
ITS QUOTE
UNQUOTE LIFE

Of course you're a Renaissance man. We're ALL Renaissance men.

She *loves* the script. Specially the dream sequence.

You're a terrorist? Thank God. I understood Meg to say you were a theorist.

And this is a 12 step program to reading an actual book.

You'll enjoy Harold, dear. He lives for the Quattrocento.

Well, I suppose it's back to good old word-of-mouth then.

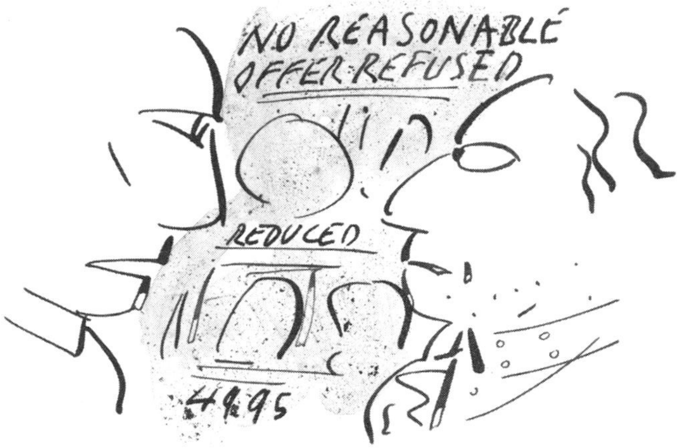
NO REASONABLE
OFFER REFUSED
REDUCED
4.95

I wish to discuss Hegel.

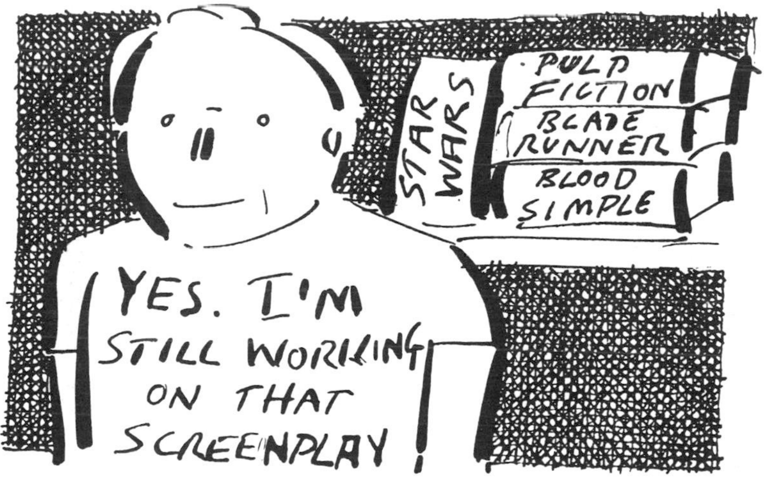
STAR WARS
PULP FICTION
BLADE RUNNER
BLOOD SIMPLE
YES. I'M STILL WORKING ON THAT SCREENPLAY!

In the Theme Park of Cultural Illusions.

Masks for the New Dramaturgy.
Post-Irony, Buddy-Buddy Movies, Sequels.

. . . and it's hard to believe but Willy is completely self-taught!

The cravat of Dr Caligari.

I thought he had a film noir sensibility. But he was just a creep.

Untitled *is* a title.

My work used to be about self-loathing. But now I'm more into narcissism.

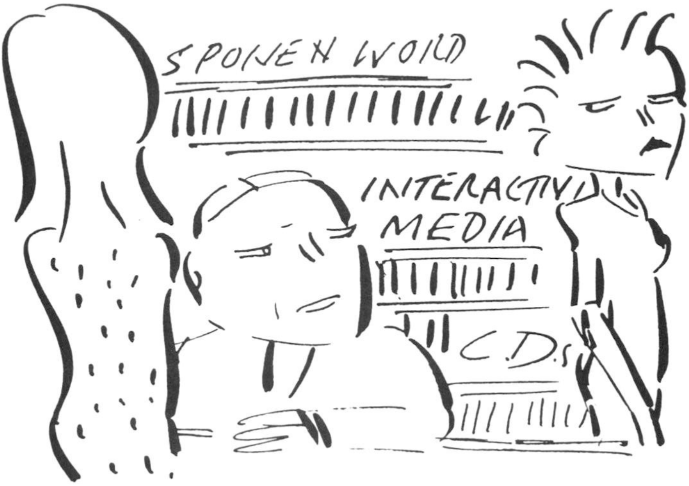
SPOKEN WORD
INTERACTIVE MEDIA
C.D.s

Books? Of course, we have books.
This is a bookstore. Um. Where do we keep the books, Clarice?

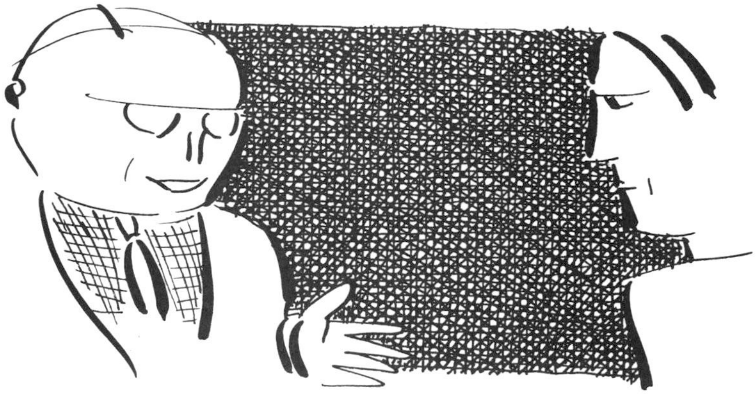

So we have your whole manuscript edited down to … drat!
Where did that little brute go?

Do you realize we may be the last generation to feel guilty
about not reading *Finnegan's Wake?*

But what I *really* want to do is direct.

I LOVED YOUR BOOK

And Other Good Stuff to Say to a Writer at a Book Party

... I saw it in Barnes & Noble and it looked great.

... I'm going to save it for a rainy day.   ... I've heard great things about it.

... Who's your agent? I've decided to write a book too.

... I thought it was a selling
review actually.

... This is the same book
you were working on five years ago?

... Who is it about?

I FOUND IT
AT THE MOVIES

Some Helpful Hints

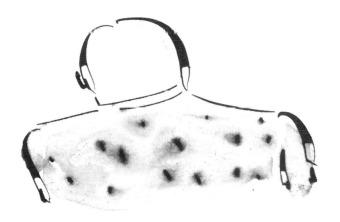

Never turn your back to the camera!

Icebergs are NOT cool.

The Devil is NOT your friend
(You'll only get burned).

Listen to that theme music.
(You may learn something!)

See Venice, and die.

Things go bump in the fog.

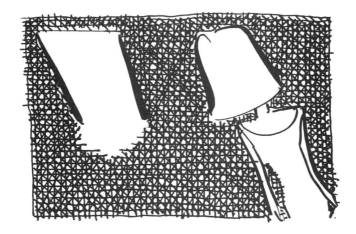

Don't go in there, silly woman!

If you pick up that hitchhiker you'll regret it to the end of your life
(which may not be much screen-time).

WHY & HOW
I MAKE MY ART

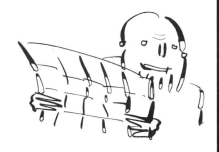

I make monochromes because
I think everybody in the world
should own a monochrome.

I am going to build
Leonardo da Vinci's helicopter
and fly it competitively.

I sabotage the whole idea
of originality. How about that?

This idea was borrowed from a *Frieze* magazine cover by David Shrigley.

I am writing an infinite sequence
of numbers but backwards!

I am investigating the entire funding
process by applying for every grant
there is under different names.
The project is going great, thanks.

I am burying myself in alluvial mud
for nine months. The piece references
Beuys, And Karen Finley, of course.

I'm a Lyrical Minimalist. Actually I had this
piece fabricated by some cartoonist
living in a *completely different dimension.*

I am making myself the most
inescapable art product on the planet.

I don't fetichize materials. I use whatever my girlfriend can shoplift.

I made a video of myself drawing
a mustache on Warhol's Blue Jackie
and rubbing it out again.

I get into gender issues by making smutty drawings in fashion magazines.

I make time-based Mimimalist pieces. It's a concept I came up with during a beef with the system over child support.

I paint. Sorry, but that's about it.

THE
RHYTHM SECTION

This is verse, not poetry. The difference is rather like the difference between cartoons and fine art, I think.

FOR A NEW YORK WOMAN: I
(She knows who she is)

Do not, please, transplant her heart
Split her genes or change her sex
Save her from interactive art
And gropers in the Cineplex

Let her dress up with great elan
But not go gaga over fashion
Let her not have a secret fan
Who loves her with a deathly passion

Keep her out of penny stocks
Or other brilliant investing
If bombings rock her, let the shocks
Be only mildly interesting

Let her be somewhat sceptical
Of scouts from Talent Agencies
May pills and powders quickly pall
Without causing dependencies

Keep strychnine from her drinking waters
Save her from earth or air pollution
Spare her from WAP. Likewise the Daughters
of the American Revolution.

Don't let her use the Internet
To bond with mooks in cyberspace
Let her at least run with a set
That know each other, face to face

Mad dog sniper on the roof
Son of God with germ or knife
She knows you had a troubled youth.
Just let her, please, get on with life.

Let her behave much as she pleases
But be particularly wary
And not pick up those foul diseases
That make this prayer so necessary

FOR A DIFFERENT NEW YORK WOMAN
(She knows who she is too)

I'll write her private number down
On public walls in loathsome places
And I will hire a circus clown
To strut behind her, making faces

I'll send her fifty Chinese dinners
I'll send cards changing her address
I'll print her name among the winners
Of some huge fictional largesse

I'll put her on the mailing lists
Of the Scientologists,
The holocaust revisionists,
And the Aesthetic Realists

I will describe her inmost dreams
On some talk show on TV
Why she's not the way she seems
Some things nobody knows but me

I'll say she's only snorting meth
Because she doesn't want to scar
And how she bores her friends to death
By whining that she's not a star

I'll have a flack announce that she'll
Soon be marrying a rat
Next day the tabloids will reveal
It's off because she got too fat

I will insert the very wildest
Photograph of her in Screw
Listen! These are just the mildest
Things that I intend to do.

FIVE IRREGULAR VERBS

To Globetrot

I am an adventurer
You are a traveller
He is a tourist
We found this wonderful unspoilt place
You came here
They have completely ruined it.

To Be Modish

I am on the Cutting Edge
You look OK, considering.
She could use help.
We are expecting a call from rather an important magazine
momentarily
You are not.
They should be getting a midnight knock on the door from the
Style Police.

To Keep Control

I am in touch with reality
You are beginning to worry me
He isn't making too much sense
We are losing it
You are out of your heads!
They are controlled by beings from another galaxy

To Love

I am head over heels in love with you
You are being evasive
He is a weasel
We are going to sort this out.
YOU DID WHAT?
They are all laughing at me

To Dine Out

I am the way I am
You are going to have to put up with me, ha-ha!
She clearly has no sense of humor
We haven't been very well seated, have we?
You are all beginning to get on my nerves
They should be taken outside and shot.

WRITING IN HAIKU

One: Looking for the Novel
I know that somewhere
The right subject is waiting.
I shall be ready.

Hello! No problem.
I'm just loaded for bear here.
Shhh … Shit! I missed it.

I sense it coming.
Gigantic, stark, luminous.
Soon I'll get started.

Two: The Novel I Wrote (compressed)
Well, hello there, Bob!
Welcome to the neighborhood
Cocktails at seven?

So it's goodbye, Bob!
We'll all have our memories
Was that his real name?

Song

Summer is icumen in
Loud sing cuckoo!
Her eggs have no albumen in
Fuck you, cuckoo!

And fuck you too, ecologist!
Neither of you will be missed.

Thinking of You

I knew a girl who sang but at the crack
Of four she got into a Cadillac
With bucket seats of coal-black leatherette

Beneath the dice that dangle in the back
Sits a fat package. I can see it sweat.

Do you like caviar? Here's enough to spread
Thick as tarred gravel on a slice of bread
The wind is moaning through the chimney flues
You put strange thoughts into a person's head

Joan a fresh blood group. Tell me all your news
Some other time. How is it, being dead?

You are going to have to put up with me, ha-ha!

EVOLUTION v. CREATION

The Debate Continues. These facts just in!

Smart deer are learning to deal with
that caught-in-headlights look!

This cat has a tenth life
fully insured!

Some dogs have their day
and their nights too!

Worms are party animals who not
only turn but do all the
new dances!

A 1950s toaster *in full working order* has been discovered just below
the so-called "fossil record" of the Pliocene Epoch!

… and Creationists are learning to fly off the Flat Earth!

3

THE GOLDEN SECTION

Celebrity is revenge!

CELEBRITY IS REVENGE

Hi! I'm the new You!

I dreamed that Cindy Crawford was on the cover of the Bible.

And now … for profound thoughts on world peace and for breaking
the $30 million per movie ceiling …

Can you imagine not even being a teeny bit famous?

Walter is at every fashionable memorial service.
He must be hugely popular amongst the dead.

Loved the buzz, hated the movie.

How George realised his new friends were really famous.

It's like that whatisname dude said.
Everybody's gonna be famous for fifteen minutes or something.

No, Frederick and I are not an item. I am an item.

... and this is Yvonne who knew me way before anybody
even guessed I was a celebrity.

Ed is doing astonishingly well. He's got his own stalker.

... and I have this terrifying premonition that
I'll be coming back as somebody called Shirley MacLaine.

DANGEROUS MINDS

A drawing of a head was sent to various inventive people, who were asked to fill them in with whatever was on their minds. This project was first done for a British magazine two years ago. It was really easy getting the heads done. Like pulling teeth from live alligators.

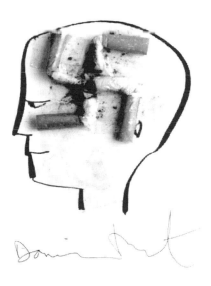

Damien Hirst, *Artist*

photograph by Shun Sasaki

SERENITY

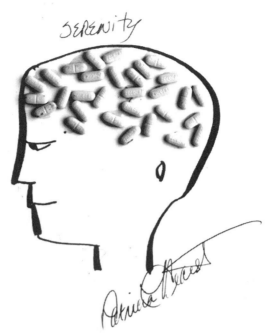

Patti Hearst, *Housewife, Actress*

Mary McFadden, *Fashion Designer*

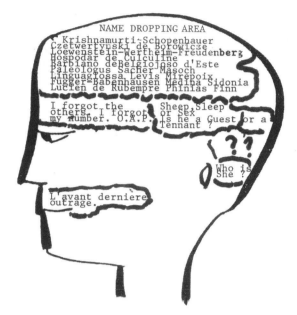

Claus von Bulow, *Retired Litigant, Memoirist*

Jay McInerney, *Novelist*

Peter Beard, *Photographer*

Andres Serrano, *Artist*

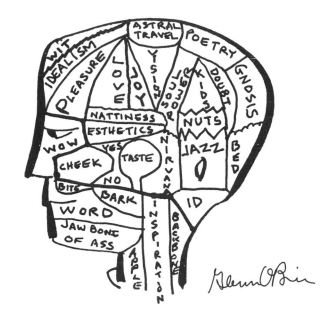

Glenn O'Brien, *Writer*

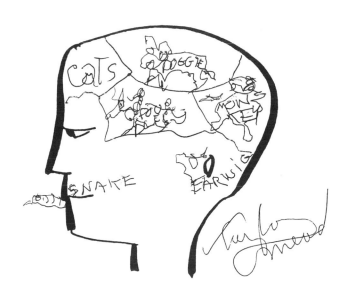

Taylor Mead, *Performer, Writer*

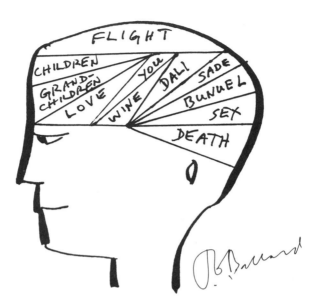

J.G. Ballard, *Novelist*

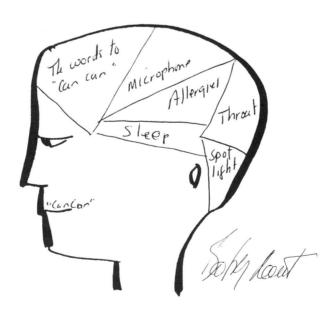

Bobby Short, *Singer*

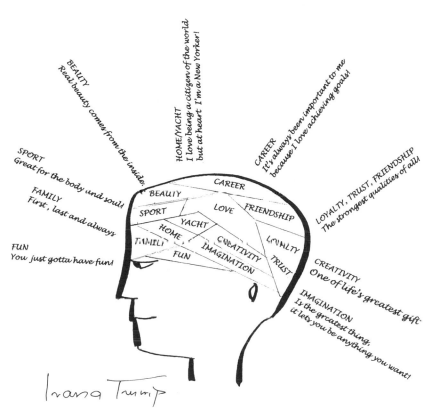

BEAUTY
Real beauty comes from the inside.

HOME/YACHT
I love being a citizen of the world
but at heart I'm a New Yorker!

CAREER
It's always been important to me
because I love achieving goals!

LOYALTY, TRUST, FRIENDSHIP
The strongest qualities of all!

SPORT
Great for the body and soul!

FAMILY
First, last and always

FUN
You just gotta have fun!

CREATIVITY
One of life's greatest gift.

IMAGINATION
Is the greatest thing;
it lets you be anything you want!

CAREER
BEAUTY
LOVE
FRIENDSHIP
SPORT
YACHT
HOME
FAMILY
CREATIVITY
LOYALTY
IMAGINATION
TRUST
FUN

Ivana Trump

Ivana Trump, *Entrepreneur*

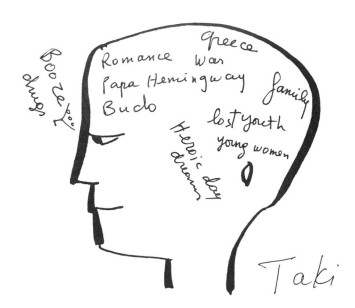

Taki Theodoracopoulos, *Columnist*

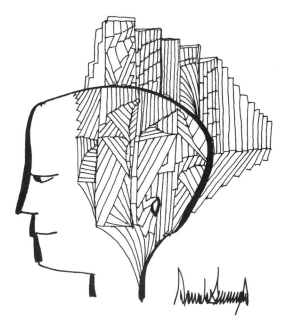

Donald Trump, *Businessman*

WHAT WERE
THEY SAYING?

The Good, The Bad and the Unbelievable

Death will be a great relief. No more interviews

Katherine Hepburn. Daily News *(New York). November 5, 1989*

Interviewer: What is your idea of perfect happiness?

Oliver Stone: Enlightenment, spiritual peace.

VF: Which historical figure do you most identify with?

Oliver Stone: Alexander the Great

VF: If you could choose how to come back, how would it be?

Oliver Stone: Not to, but if i must, a tortured beggar in Calcutta.

Excerpts from an interview in Vanity Fair *December 1993*

Imagine meeting *me* here!

*Artist, movie-maker Julian Schnabel to photographer Jessica Craig-Martin
on the beach in Mexico in the mid 90s.*

It would be unfair to write Elisabeth off in terms of this picture.
I think people should be a little bit more compassionate.
I have a script at Savoy called Foreplay that I think she would be perfect for.

*Joe Esterhas talks to Los Angeles Times about actress Elisabeth Berkley
after the* Showgirls *fiasco. Savoy, sadly, is no longer with us.*

My knee is my Achilles heel.

Sylvia MIles, actress (Heat, *etc.*) *to AHG in late 90s.*

People have public lives and private lives. And sometimes they have secret lives.

TV sportscaster Marv Albert during his trial for forced sex which detailed his taste for cross-dressing. Albert—who, perhaps by coincidence, was quoting Gabriel Garcia Marques— lost, but is back at NBC. New York Daily News. *September 23, 1997.*

Television has changed. Standards have gone down to an all-time low and I'm here to represent it. It's a miracle. I prayed to God for this.

Howards Stern at the launch of his TV show. New York Times. *April 2, 1998. The show tanked.*

I have enough trouble with what I have.

Sharon Stone, responding to the suggestion that her liking for firearms indicated a Freudian penis envy. Newsweek, *May 6, 1998.*

Valuation is often not a helpful tool in determining when to sell hypergrowth stocks.

Henry Blodgett, Merrill Lynch's celebrity Internet analyst,
in a report, published January 10, 2000.

Mother Teresa never quit in a down quarter and what we're doing is equally important. In this particular case, it's just a down day.

Michael Saylor, CEO of MicroStrategy, the software manufacturer, after losing
$6 billion in one day. The New York Daily News. *March 21, 2000.*

Do not provoke a snake before you make up your mind
and summon up the ability to cut off its head.

Saddam Hussein, London Observer, August 2000

Why would anybody buy a Picasso?
It's going to be worthless – by the year 2020 Picasso will be a joke.

Tom Wolfe, reacting to S.I. Newhouse's purchase of a painting.
New York Daily News. *May 26, 2000.*

It's not the idea. It's the check.

Gene Simmons, bandleader of Kiss, when presented with the suggestion the band name be used to sell a beer cooler shaped like a coffin. The New York Times. *June 17, 2001.*

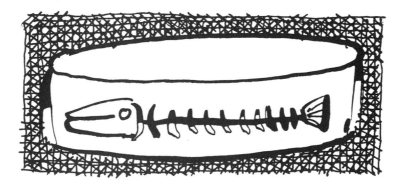

The Caspian … is not half-empty; it's half-full.

Armen Petrossian, president of the International Caviar Importers, responding to reports that stocks of Caspian Sea sturgeon had been depleted by perhaps 90 percent in the last two decades. The New York Times. *June 21, 2001.*

… that's not a big procedure. That's real simple, nothing … When they cut
you open they stick a probe in there, like, and they suck the fat out.
And then there's nothing left. It's nice and clean in there. And they cut it and
stretch it. By the time you wake up, it's done.

*Salvatore "Sammy Bull" Gravano talking about his face-lift to fellow rat "Fat Dom" Borghese.
On federal wiretaps, published July 1, 2001.*

If you're feeling full of yourself and enjoying the moment and everyone's telling you
how wonderful you are – I mean, you just go with it until you realize and grow up.

*Linda Evangelista, August 2001, explaining her comment – a comment that helped capsize the
Supermodel phenomenon – that "I don't get out of bed for less than $10,000 a day."*
The Today Show. *August 23, 2001.*

My Lord, in this place, all you have to do is think about something, and it's leaked.
It's like there are eavesdropping microphones on your brain.

Donald Rumsfeld to Time, *August 27, 2001.*

If Madonna cuts her hair, we'll get it into the magazine right away,
instead of having to wait for the November issue of *Vogue.*

Brandusa Niro, editor of Style 24/7, *on September 4, 2001, the day before
the launch of the fashion-and-celebrity magazine.*

We only did half the book and we have the second half still to film.
It's really a nuts-and-bolts thing. If the studio makes enough money, then they'll
do it, so we'll have to see how profitable *Battlefield Earth* turns out to be.

John Travolta. The Daily Telegraph *(London), June 28, 2001.*

By preserving these unique sites, we share our culture and rich diversity
with our children for future generations.

*Gale Norton, Interior Secretary, in an August 2001 release naming the Fresno
Sanitary Landfill as a historic landmark. It was soon learned that the
Environmental Protection Agency had listed the dump as a toxin-leaking threat.*

Man, that is impossible—I throw all my clothes out after I wear them once.

Sean Combs to Milanese club-owner Ivano Fatibene, responding to the vile suggestion that he had worn the same suit twice. Page Six, New York Post. *August 20, 2001.*

I'm a movie star. Can I talk to my entertainment lawyer?

*Natasha Lyonne, 22 year old actress (*American Pie 2*), to a Miami Beach cop after running her rented Dodge into a traffic sign. August 28, 2001.*

The action against the World Trade Center was … the greatest work of art ever.

Karlheinz Stockhausen at a press conference before the Hamburg Music Festival, September 2001. The composer had concerts cancelled. A frantic Stockhausen claimed that he had meant to call it "The Devil's artwork" but he was roundly trashed for "aestheticising terror" by other artists, including Richard Serra.

It's as though it's 1937 and I'm a band leader named Freddie Hitler. Maybe we should change the name now. A friend suggested "Basket of Puppies." People keep coming up to me and saying "Hey, wouldn't it be funny if you got anthrax?" I'm like, "Oh, that'd be hilarious." I will not die a post-ironic death.

Scott Ian, lead singer of the heavy metal band, Anthrax, pointing out that he had acquired some Cipro. The Reliable Source, The Washington Post, October 10, 2001. Many in the immediate aftermath of the attack predicted the end of Irony and Fluff. But Irony and Fluff are hardy growths — as hardy as the culture that produced them.

INSIDE THE
MEDIA CONSPIRACY

So the question is … do people not in the media actually exist?

Borrring! Nothing but news in the papers these days

Welcome to Reality Cartooning! We are keeping nine people in this panel –
without a punchline between them. Hilarious!

Is that "No comment! meaning yes, "No Comment" meaning no,
or "No comment" meaning up yours?

Secret messages and paranoid delusions in the media as usual.

Hello, sweetheart. Get me the Style section.

Okay. Any volunteers to be the Innocent Bystander?

Apparently the Internet killed the media star.

That's odd. Everybody so adored the party.

WHAT THEY SAY
& WHAT THEY MEAN

In The Tabloids

A Recluse: Somebody who doesn't go to restaurant openings.

A Legend: A geezer.

A legendary recluse: A geezer who won't take our calls.

"He was a quiet person":
The larval phase of a multiple homicide.

"He was a friendly person who believed in the American dream."
One of the victims of the above-named quiet person.

A Wild Child: A perp with rich or famous parents.

A Living Hell: A nasty situation one of our by-lines heard
about in a bar and can do an eye-witness on.

Charismatic: Not always rude, hideous or disgusting.

A Hero: Somebody who has not been videotaped taking bribes.

A Fiend: Somebody who is dead meat upon meeting a hero.

PERFORMER
ANXIETIES

... but I thought you said this was just a dress rehearsal.

Personally je regrette beaucoup!

… but then I found yes, yes, they COULD take that away from me,

Wrong! Most businesses are like show business.

Unfortunately everybody knows the trouble I've seen.

4

THE WAY

WE LIVE NOW

Brooke always wanted to be somebody.
Now she wants to be somebody else.

THE LETTER

THIS LETTER HAS BEEN SENT TO YOU FOR LUCK!! PLEASE
SEND IT TO 20 PEOPLE. IT MUST LEAVE YOUR HANDS
IN 4 DAYS. OTTO BRUNER OF CHICAGO   SENT IT
                          AND SOON INHERITED   AN
ANCIENT SCOTTISH TITLE!!!
GEORGE PUGH OF TUXEDO PARK   SCOFFED
AT THE LETTER. THREE GENTLEMEN   FROM
BROOKLYN MISTOOK HIM FOR A STOOLIE. EDDIE

BROWN FROM NORTH LONDON
ACCIDENTALLY THREW IT AWAY. HE WENT   MAD.
HIS TWIN BROTHER ARTHUR FOUND IT AND POSTED IT. HE
DISCOVERED THE UNIFIED THEORY OF BEING!!! EMMA
EARLY OF CORK   SENT IT.   SHE
AWORE A   NATURAL
BLONDE AND HER NEIGHBOUR'S
ANNOYING DOG DIED. HER COUSIN ERIN   IGNORED
IT & BECAME THE TARGET OF VICIOUS GOSSIP! EUNICE
PLUM OF SEATTLE   FORGOT IT
AND   GOT A   VERY HEAVY
                  COLD.

HER HUSBAND NORTON THREW IT AWAY AND WAS BITTEN
BY A DEADLY SNAKE IN A PRODUCE STORE. EUNICE SENT
IT & MADE OUT LIKE A BANDIT ON THE LIFE INSURANCE!!!

BUSINESS BRAINS

Troubling news, B D. They found a loophole in our loophole.

As your legal team, BD, we feel your two best options are sudden, humiliating exposure or the slow unraveling of a pathetic cover-up.

Oh, nothing much. Waiting for a couple of major deals to fall through. And you?

Thanks, Ed. It's heart-warming how folks rally around when you're back on top.

So, gentlemen, we are agreed!
As a routine business precaution we whack all the witnesses.

Getting downsized hasn't been all bad.
At least it's given me time to work on my Enemies List.

Of course I always talk about money.
That's the only way I can get anybody to listen.

And a toast to JJ. For charging clients billable hours for the office party.

No. Frankly I was thinking how small and insignificant *they* are.

I was a corporate raider before it was fashionable,
I was a corporate raider while it was fashionable and I am *still* a corporate raider.

Graham is the family intellectual.
He handles the philanthropy and makes the bad investments.

Great résumé. But frankly I don't see how you would fit into our corporate culture.

FOR SOME REASON SIMON'S NORMAL SUPERB COMMUNICATIONS SKILLS BETRAYED HIM THAT WHOLE LONG FRUSTRATING DAY

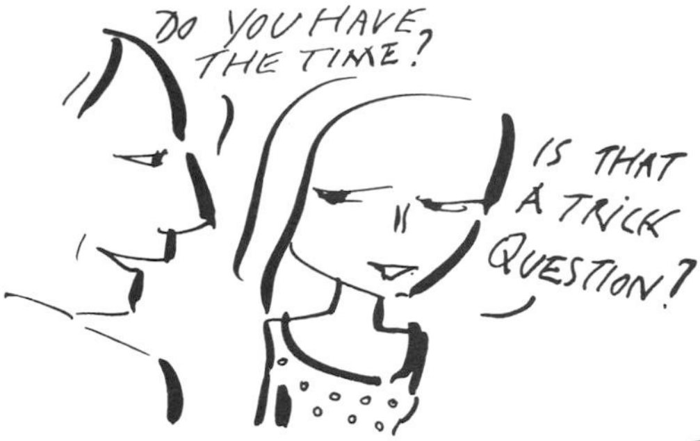
DO YOU HAVE THE TIME?
IS THAT A TRICK QUESTION?

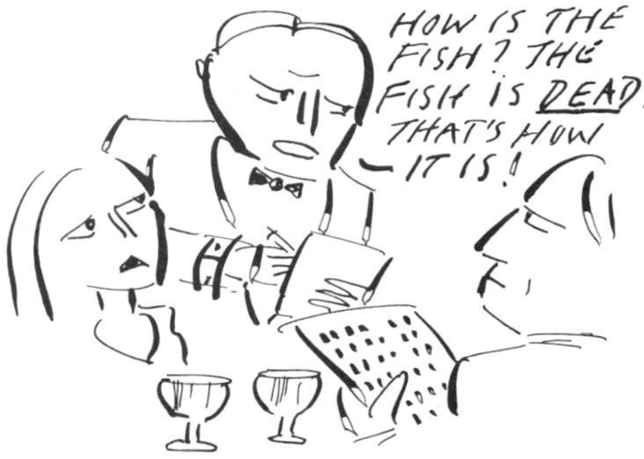
HOW IS THE FISH? THE FISH IS DEAD! THAT'S HOW IT IS!

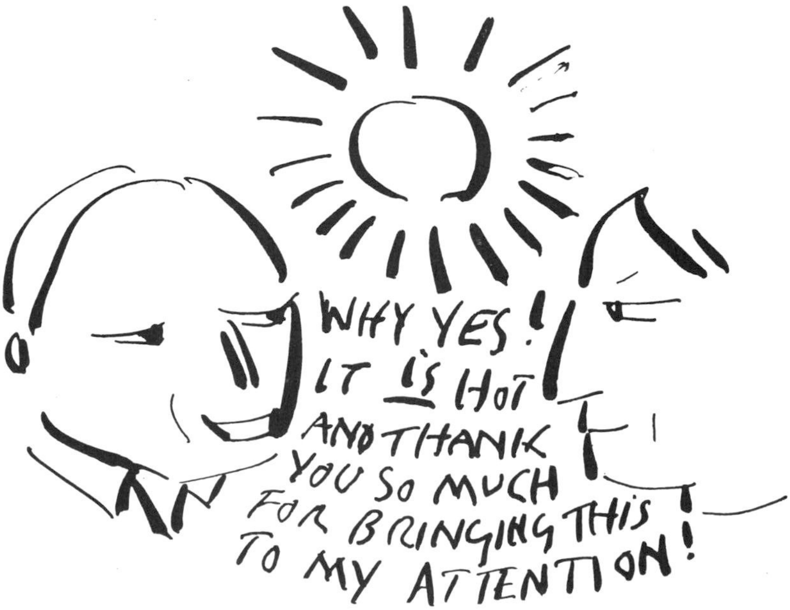
WHY YES! IT IS HOT AND THANK YOU SO MUCH FOR BRINGING THIS TO MY ATTENTION!

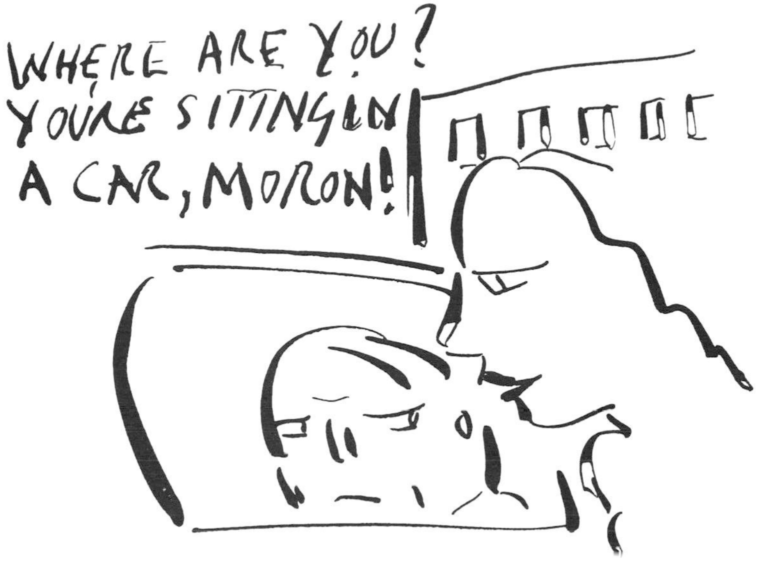
WHERE ARE YOU? YOU'RE SITTING IN A CAR, MORON!

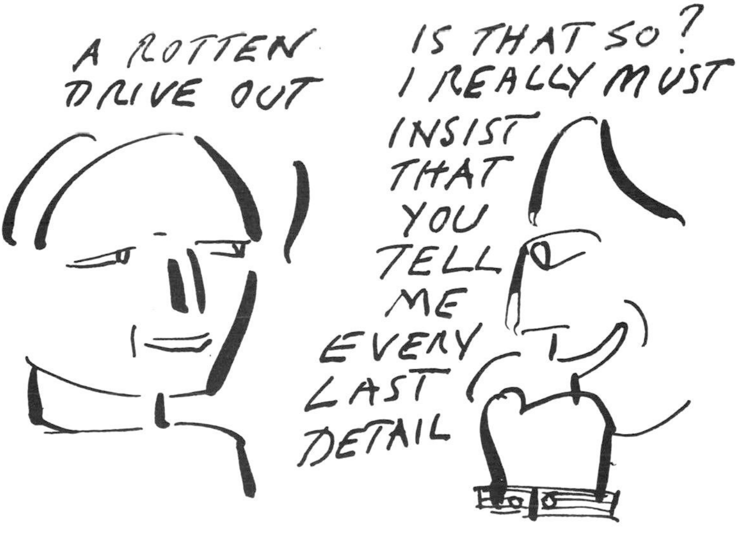
A ROTTEN DRIVE OUT
IS THAT SO? I REALLY MUST INSIST THAT YOU TELL ME EVERY LAST DETAIL

FAMILY FUN

… and this is my wife, Katherine,
who is attractive and successful in her own right.

Of course I still love you! Don't we go to Events?

... and then the prince killed the giant and kissed the Sleeping Great Personality

Who are you going to believe, honey-pie?
Some silly old gossip column or me?

At last! The shortest fairy tale in the world.

Don't answer. It might be somebody.

… and this is my biological cousin, Chester.

Amanda says she has given herself permission not to be perfect, dear.

Don't be so naïve, Felicia. To you, it's porn. To me, it's research material.

... and here's grandpa, being inducted into the Rock 'n' Roll Hall of Fame.

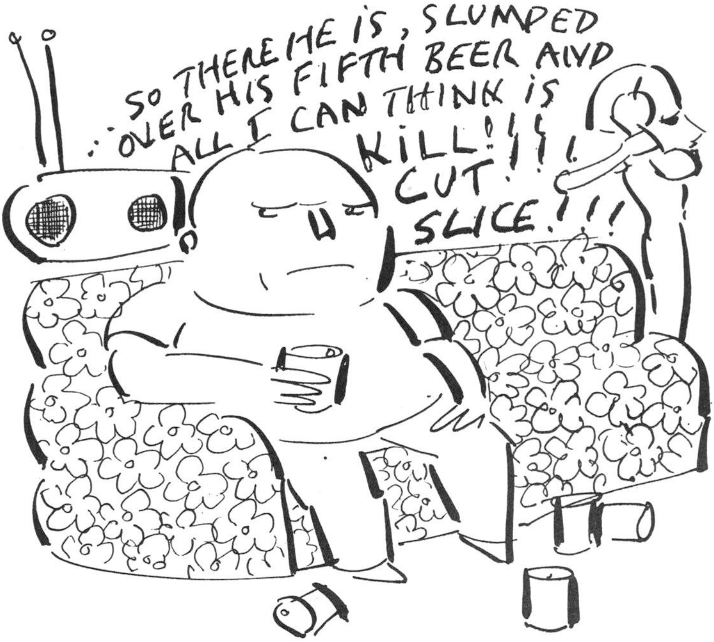
...SO THERE HE IS, SLUMPED OVER HIS FIFTH BEER AND ALL I CAN THINK IS
KILL!!!
CUT!!!
SLICE!!!

But I *am* taking charge of my life. I'm hooking.

But it was only because he reminded me so much of you,
darling, except with a sense of humor.

I know you follow a different drummer. But,
sweetheart, it seems to be always a *different* different drummer.

Then he did get all the toxins out of his system.
And there was so little left I divorced him.

HIS 'N' HERS DOORMATS

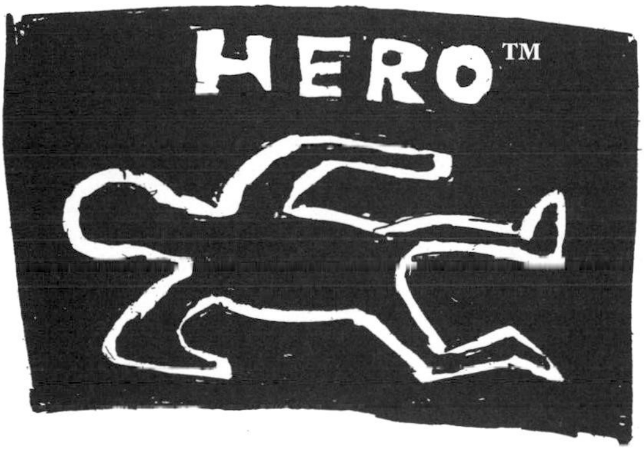
HERO™

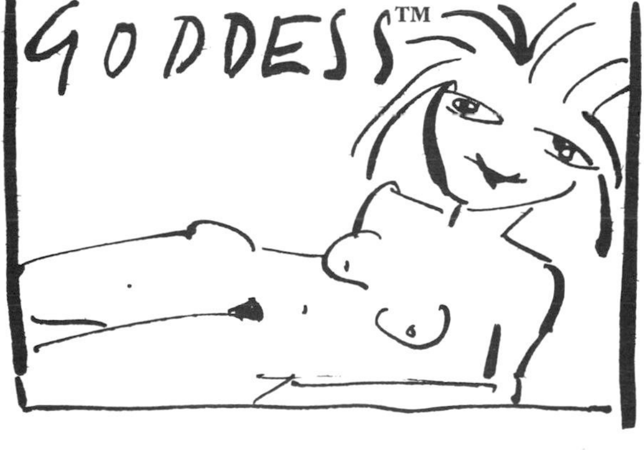
GODDESS™

WHAT SHE SAYS
& WHAT SHE MEANS

You're looking prosperous.
(You're looking fat).

An idea of that inimitable caricaturist, the late Mark Boxer

You're looking good.
(You're looking old).

You're looking *great!*
(I thought you were dead).

MODERN MANNERS

Up the Down Staircase.

I then realized I had lost the respect of my peers.
So I got a fresh set of peers.

You're too late. There's absolutely nobody left.

Even I don't like you, Ed. And I'm your *best friend*.

How do you mean I look in bad shape?
I happen to be a member of four rather exclusive health clubs.

Hi! It's us! The same old familiar faces!

Well if it isn't you who's dead – who is it?

Of course, I've been talking about you behind your back.
What are backs for?

But why shouldn't I lie? It's the only thing I do well.

Actually, Zoe is her club name. Her cult name is Emmeline, her pseudonym is Marguerite and her hurricane name is Fred.

Is that tobacco I smell in your joint, young man?

I used to treat my body like a temple.
Now I treat it more like a drive-in.

Lucius is utterly and completely rotten. But Old School rotten.

Velma and Eddie are huge in the demi-monde, dear.

Well, they don't look like they're chirping to ME.

Well, yes. That is my *calendar* age.
I took ten years off for good behaviour.

That evening Wally and Tod realised the era of the dot coms
was well and truly over.

Of course, you're basically very shy.
We're all basically very shy.

I don't get it.
Why *shouldn't* I join a club that lets in people like me?

I am on the cutting edge. Avril makes the scene. Kurt is fabulous.
Quite honestly we don't see where you would fit in, Ted.

That'll be quite enough debonair persiflage out of you, stranger.

Aha! Wild animals! I scented you from across the room!

If we'd known you were so amusing
we would have invited somebody with a sense of humor.

Great acoustics! I can't hear a thing.

You know I would never lie, Bob. Except to women, of course.

Of course, I can keep secrets.
It's the people I tell them to that can't keep secrets.

You don't have a life, Bob. But that's okay. Not many people do.

Oh, excuse me! Did you think I was paying attention?

Sadly, the attempt to bring realism to Commercial Sex was a failure.

Just ignore Katy. New faces make her timid.

I may be a rich girl. But I too hear the song of the streets.

There you are, Bob! We were just talking about you.

I remember when Julia and I were the same age.

Don't mention it doesn't mean thanks for mentioning it.
It means DON'T MENTION IT!

Max says he's walked the walk, he's talked the talk,
and now he's going to drink the drink.

No, that's HH's grand-daughter.
But you're right. She is young enough to be his wife.

It's a terrific weight-loss program except you turn into an anorexic teen-age girl.

We're so impressed by how virile you are
in not caving in to that anti-smoking nonsense.

Courtney's a rich girl with no money.

Now it's Mona saying she's very, very, very happy.
I tell you — there's something spooky going on around here,

But we've never been anywhere we've never been.

I don't have to pay my dues. Daddy already paid them.

... and to Lloyd, who was looking forward to being mentioned in my will.
Hi, Lloyd!

WHAT THEY SAY
& WHAT THEY MEAN

At a Cocktail Party

What a pleasant surprise.
(You get asked out? Amazing!)

An idea of that inimitable caricaturist, the late Mark Boxer

I love to watch people at parties.
(Nobody talks to me at parties)

I've been trying to get in touch with you
for ages. (I just gave a party and
I didn't invite *you*?)

Call me.
(Don't think about it)

You look mysterious.
(You look pretentious)

Have you known our hosts long?
(Who let you in?)

e-Answered Prayers

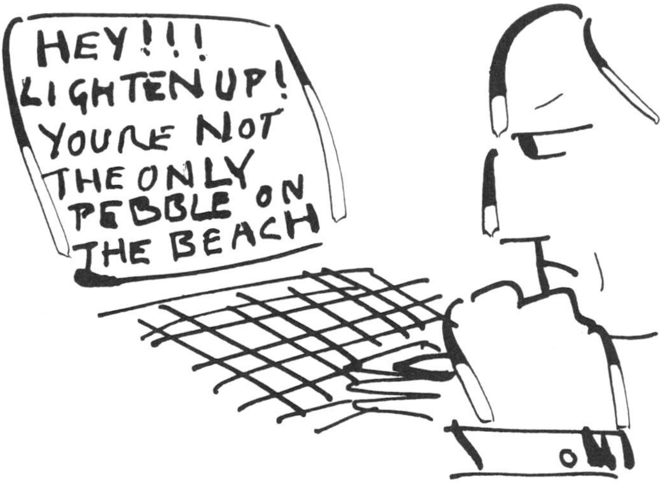
HEY!!!
LIGHTEN UP!
YOURE NOT
THE ONLY
PEBBLE ON
THE BEACH

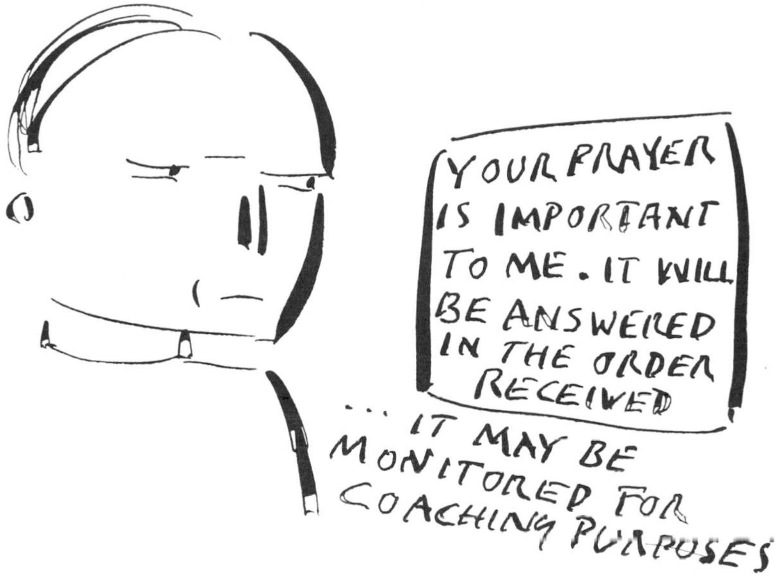
YOUR PRAYER IS IMPORTANT TO ME. IT WILL BE ANSWERED IN THE ORDER RECEIVED
... IT MAY BE MONITORED FOR COACHING PURPOSES

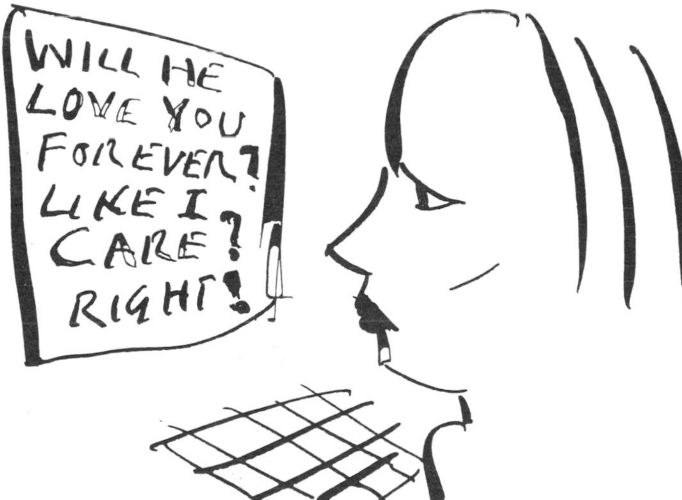
WILL HE LOVE YOU FOREVER? LIKE I CARE? RIGHT!

...THINGS ARE NEVER AS BAD AS THEY SEEM...

A SMILE IS NATURE'S BEST MEDICINE

...EVERY CLOUD HAS A SILVER LINING...

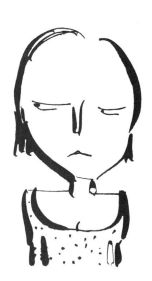

I'LL BE GETTING BACK TO YOU ON THAT. OK?

NOTES TOWARD
A NEW ETIQUETTE

Do not wear dark glasses at night unless you have
a contagious eye disease.

Do not use slang or foul language in the presence of your juniors.
You will only get it wrong and embarrass yourself.

For The Post Young
Do not be hip.

For The Young
Do not be cool.

Sorry, but spelling your first name wrong
is *not* a creative act.

On Being a Gentleman

Women and children first! Especially when losing height in a balloon
or when food runs short during a war alert.

On Being a Lady
Be sensitive but honest. And if they can't take it, screw 'em!

On Sexual Mores
Do not betray the secrets of the Heart. Until the check clears anyway.

On Service
Do not call waiters or taxidrivers "Sir"
unless you expect *them* to tip *you*.

On Birthdays
Do not allow yours to be celebrated in public by a chorus
of waiters if you don't want your fellow diners to wish you had never been born.

In General

Amusing people do not have amusing messages on their
answering machines, witty people seldom wear witty T-shirts, and you
very seldom get fascinating e-mails from people with fascinating lives.

Whoever thinks nobody notices he is wearing a hairpiece
can't be trusted about anything else either.

Avoid cannibalism and other fad diets.

Do not high-five the Almighty.

THE CLASS-WAR
OF WORDS

It began when a couple of T-shirts made an unprovoked
assault on a cushion in Pasadena, California.

A gang of cushions struck back, cornering an unwary
T-shirt that had strayed onto Manhattan's Upper East Side.

Which was when guerrilla groups of bumper-stickers
from the Mountain States saw their chance!

The conflict escalated when posse of T-shirts
from South Beach engaged with the Palm Beach cushion colony.
(To be continued. Maybe.)

NORMAL PEOPLE!

Journeys Into (Other People's) Space

Normal people? Normal people are just people
you don't know very well.

I'm afraid Magda isn't quite as amusing as people think.

Bruno spurned conventional success
but made a brilliant career as a renaissance failure.

That's perfectly OK, Bob. If I were you I'd feel desperate too.

I can't get a *job*, Maria. For goodness sake, I've got far too much to do.

Harry believes every single word he hears. He's such a cynic.

We see Olivia as a force of nature. Fog.

Fine, thanks. Just my usual state of raging panic.

Remember, Butch. Exam results aren't everything.
They just let people know who's stupid.

… and then when I came off my medication
I realized what street signs really *mean*.

It's not so much that Emma loves animals.
It's more a message she's sending to people.

I'm afraid we don't like food that's more interesting than we are.

Marianne says yes to life. But she says no to everything else.

Just who are you calling overbearing, pal?

Oh, that's Deedee. She's so darling.
We call her The Destroyer. But very, very playfully.

Keith is a lost soul. That's so romantic!

I'd explain the joke. But then we would have to kill you.

Then I got to wondering … down these mean streets why *should* I go?

I fear that Minnie's divorce from reality is final.

Morning after morning Eliot was forced to face the same agonizing choices.

Tom's gone mad. It's the smartest thing he has done in years.

SOME HIGHLY ENDANGERED
HUMAN SPECIES

The Conservative who likes to conserve stuff

The Utopian.
Welcome to the City of the Future!

The Lyric Poet
My muse said be a ghostwriter but then
said forget it! You ARE a ghost writer.

The Supermodel.
… then this sweet Italian pharmaceuticals tycoon
paid $250,000 for a one time use of an X-ray of my pelvis!

The Explorer
When there were still Theres *There*!

The Photo-Journalist
So I dug up some old shot from an archive, colorised
it, digitised in background from Bosnia or Beirut or Kabul or
wherever and … hey! The Disasters of War! Pulitzer time!

The Rock Scholar

The Cinephile
Who knows everything about Truffaut, Antonioni and
Kurosawa except their opening week-end grosses

CLOSER TO THE EDGE

You miss so much these days if you stop to think.

Well, if we can't talk you out of it, can we at least webcast it?

Greetings, casual bystanders! I am a disgruntled former postal worker.

Are you receiving me? In the Middle way of life
I found myself in a dark wood. Over.

Excellent! I see the Fat Lady is about to sing.

How do you mean this isn't brain surgery, doctor? It IS brain surgery.

But just suppose we're not living in a movie but in a movie-within-a-movie?

It's a conspiracy so immense that we may all be part of it.

That was Henry's last breath.

Of course it worked like a charm. It *was* a charm.

Then Greg's personal demon bonded with Horace's personal demon
and things took a turn for the worse.

But I wouldn't be telling you all this if you were actually here.

Hubley had never believed in visions until he saw Madonna
with the Madonna after his third jug of pina colada.

You see! It actually IS thicker than water!

We're supposed to be post-ironical, Fred. We're not supposed to be dumb.

I have the funniest feeling we shouldn't have eaten the free lunch.

Wendell believes we are targeted by the World Government, Joan believes that
Hollywood is controlled by Satanists, I believe Washington DC is populated by
an alien race. How come you don't believe in anything, George?

Warning signs that a loved one may have got involved with a cult.

I *know* these are the Last Days. Does that mean I can't have a bit of fun?

665

Uh- oh! Things are looking tricky.
That's the Sign of the Beast's next door neighbor.

Unfortunately even this is a lie.

It says I'm going on early to avoid the rush.

HAPPY ENDINGS

Blueprint for An End-of-the-World-as-We-Know-It game.
(Still working on the rules!)

You have entered the realm of Virtual Reality. You can't get into a
Virtual Co-Op. You are not allowed in the Virtual Beach Club.
Your name is spelled wrong in a Virtual gossip column.

You see a silver spaceship fly in the yellow rays of dawn.
You see a silver spaceship in the dying rays of the sun.
You see a killer asteroid headed in the same direction.
Oops!

Tell-tale signs that you have entered the Realm of a Mad Dictator!

You learn that the resort you went to as a child had once been used for
military research. It was nicknamed Bio Beach.

Welcome to the Universal Mall. A McDonalds has been ambushed,
the opening of a blockbuster was smoke-bombed in the megaplex
and a sweatshop has been discovered beneath a sportswear outlet but
don't worry! Globalization is in almost complete control.

Arcadia is not dead! You just got here. Quit while you're ahead.

The program for picking up intelligent transmissions from Outer Space
gets a call. It's for you! The call is collect. Your temp refuses to take it.
Whoever is Out There calls back. It's a prank caller from another galaxy!
Your recorder was on the fritz. Not even the tabs believe you.

TOMORROW'S SPECIALS

You have had yourself cloned. A batch of you has been cryogenically frozen and laid down in storage. Will you be part the future ruling elite or the future food supply? Bet you all can't wait to find out!

You are in the Land of Cockayne. Do what you want is the only law! Everything looks, smells and tastes delicious! Sexual desires are always at their peak! But it's all happening next door.

You found a Doomsday Cult. Your temple is in Malibu. The Malibu Colony is stricken by a hurricane, brushfires, mudslides and a Tsunami. You become a Hollywood god. Converts flock to you from distant lands.

Welcome to the Badlands. Nihilists creep through the sand dunes. Paramilitaries squelch through the sleet. Agents in dark glasses surround the jungle perimeter. Now what?

The woman with the vat of cyanide runs into a jogger with a rifle at the reservoir. Next morning the man with the bottled sarin gas pours himself a glass of water before heading for the subway.

A powerful new study proves that global warming is not really happening. Also that over population is no problem. Also that most species aren't actually endangered—just nervous. The research was done by the Tooth Fairy.

Congratulations! You are the first human to have caught a computer virus. Major, major commercial possibilities here.

Somebody spots you in a supermarket. It's Elvis!! He sings you a new song. It will save rock-and-roll. You hear a catchy bit of Muzak walking to the car-park and forget it.

ARMAGEDDON AND THE NEW ECONOMY

The Lord of the Flies is a keynote speaker at the World Economic Forum.
The Fates show up at Bohemian Grove. Kali is booked for a G8 meeting,
The Exterminating Angel is a guest of Herbert Allen's at Sun Valley and
Disney and AOL-Time Warner squabble over the merchandizing.

Genetically modified trees have saved the rainforest. Unfortunately THEY hug YOU.